Nap Time!

by Carmel Reilly

illustrated by Ruth Bennett

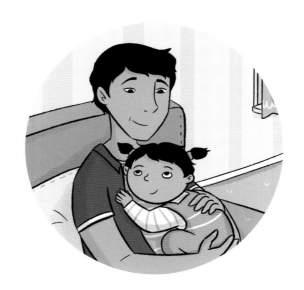

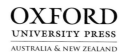

OXFORD
UNIVERSITY PRESS
AUSTRALIA & NEW ZEALAND

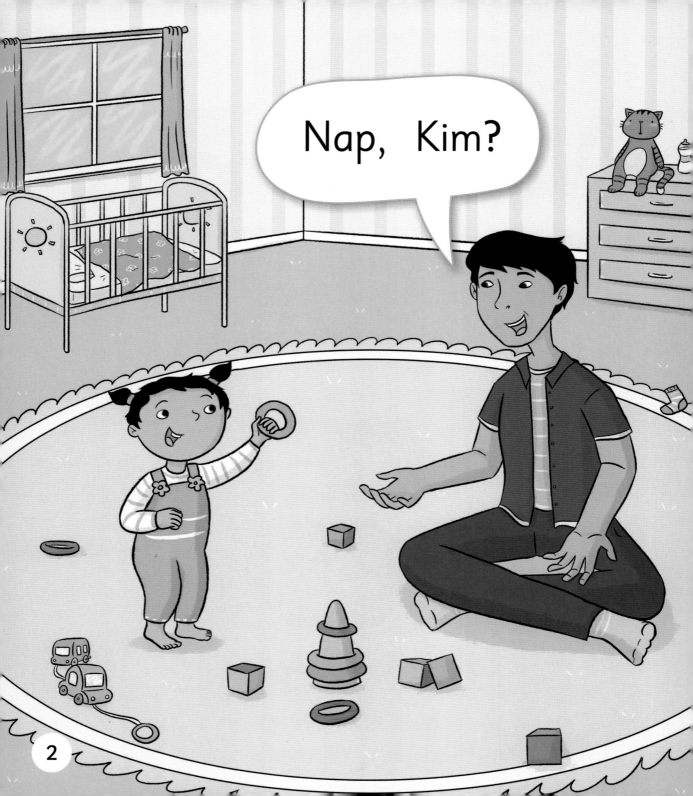

Kim got in a cot.

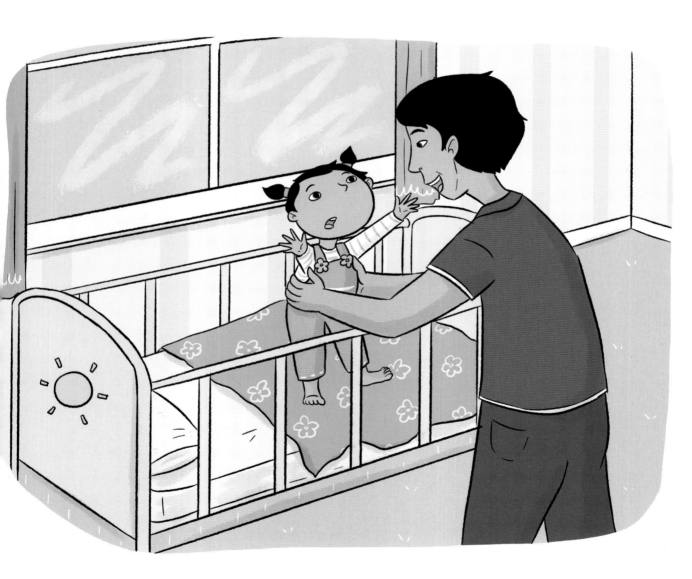

Kim sat in a cot.

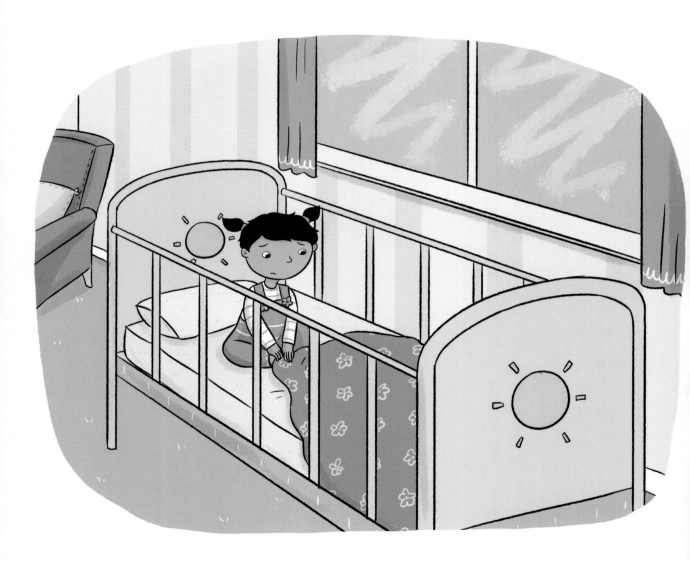

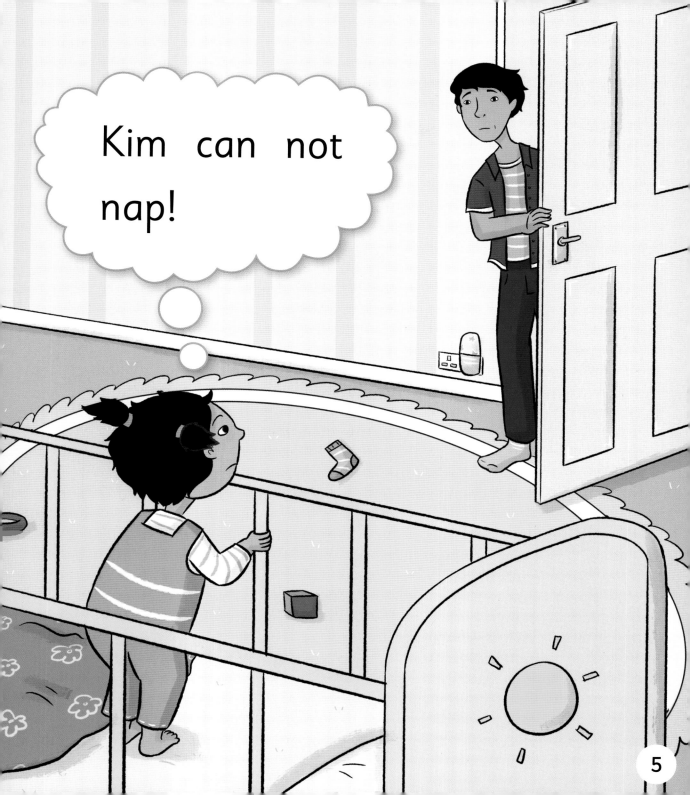

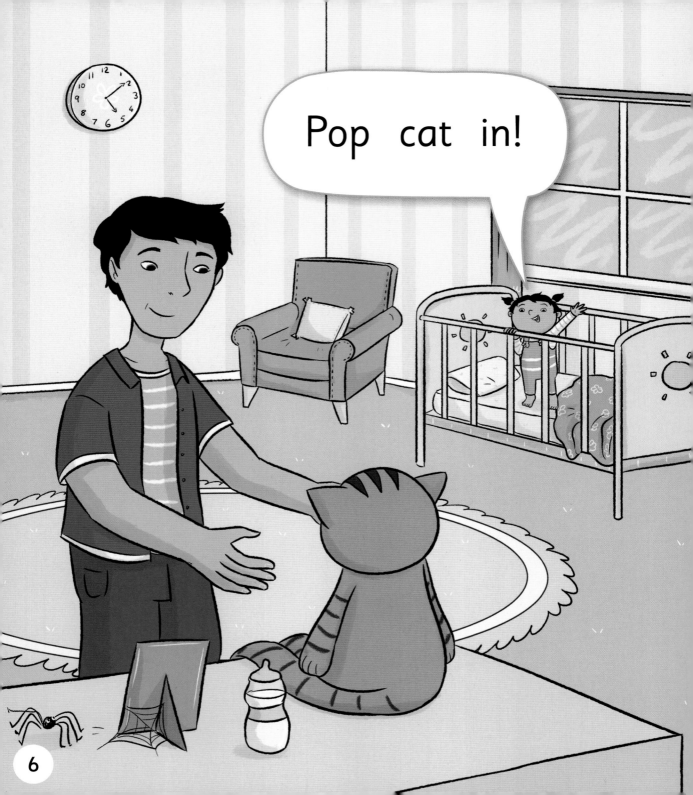

Dad got cat.

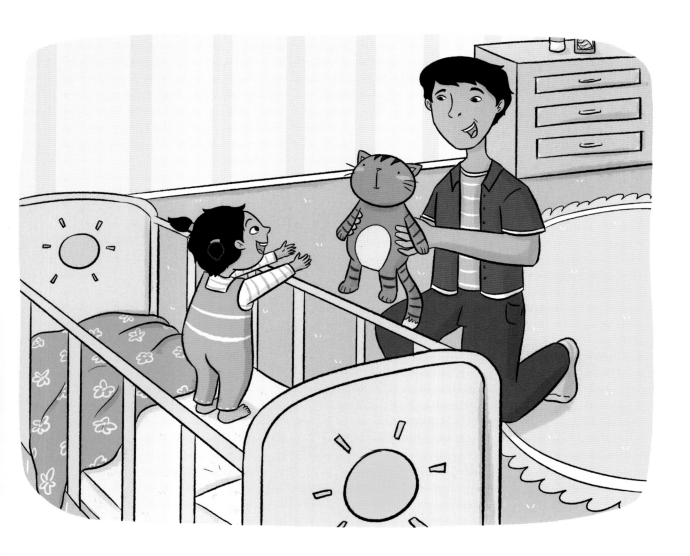

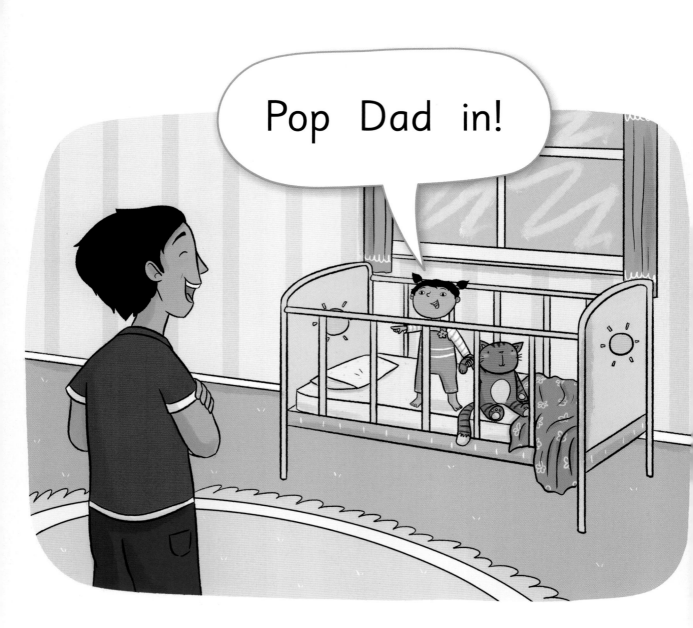

Dad sat.

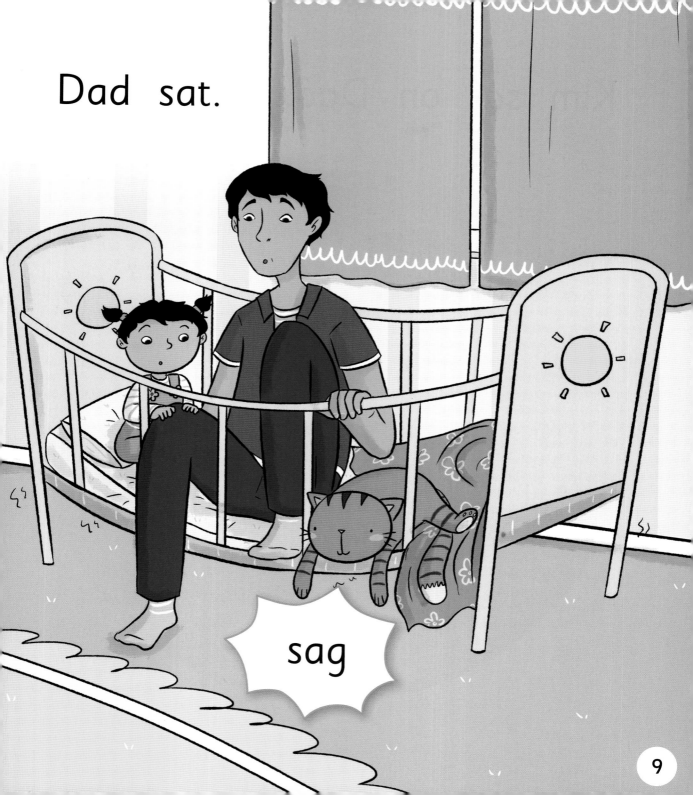

sag

Kim sat on Dad.

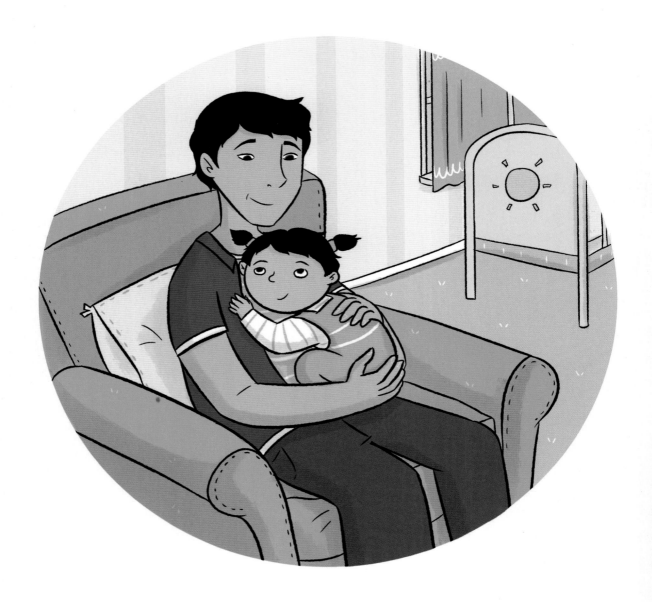

Cat sat on Kim.

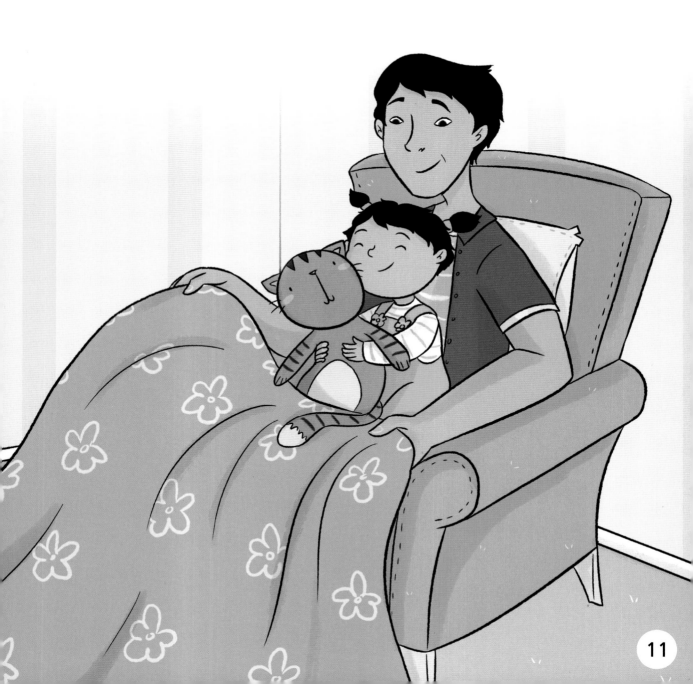

Kim and Dad nap.

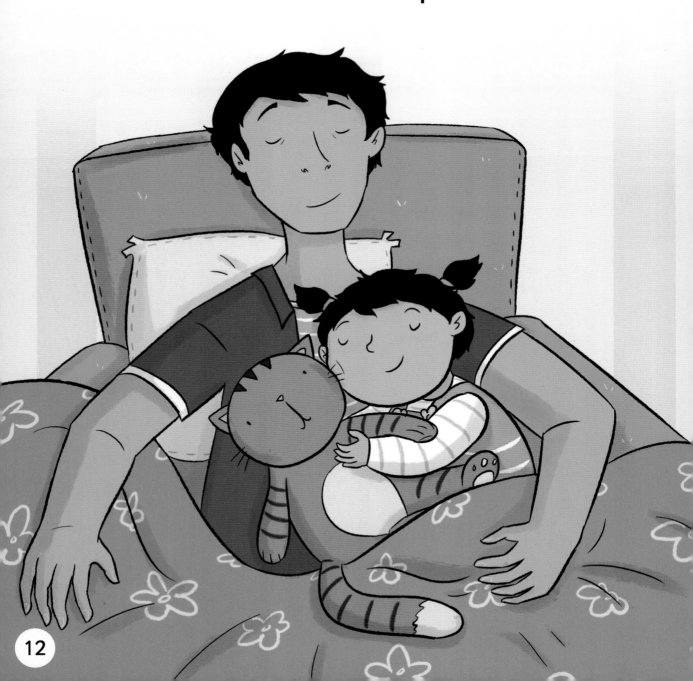